Plant Milk Power

Plant Milk Power

Dairy-free drinks that are good for your body and the planet

Deborah Kaloper

Harper *by* Design

Introduction 7

Basics 17

Cold 29

Hot 65

Boozy 85

Index 105

5

Contents

Introduction

This is a recipe book for alt-milk enthusiasts who want to experiment with different plants, grains, nuts and seeds to create a range of delicious vegan beverages. It is also for anyone who is curious about taking another step into the world of plant-forward thinking, drinking and eating. Plant-based and plant-forward diets are not exclusive to vegans or vegetarians—they are for anyone wanting a healthier and more sustainable lifestyle.

Plant-based milks are not a fad. They have been used in many cultures around the world for centuries: Soy milk is recorded as being used in China as early as 1365 CE, and almond milk makes an appearance in an Egyptian cookery book from the 14th century.

These days, our increased awareness of general health and wellness, and environmental and ethical concerns, has many of us looking to the beneficial powers of dairy-free alternatives. Enthusiasts are also driven by the wide variety of taste and flavour profiles of different plant milks ... why settle for one dairy alternative when there is an abundance of choice on the supermarket shelves, and even more to choose from when you start blending and creating your own milks at home?

Homemade plant milk lets you have complete control over what you're drinking. Most commercially produced milks contain fillers such as oil, excess sugar and preservatives, but when you blend your own milk, you know exactly what goes into it. It's also incredibly simple and economical to make plant-based milk at home. All the base milk recipes in this book contain just a few simple ingredients: plants, grains, seeds, legumes or nuts, and water.

Adding salt, sweetener and spices for flavour is totally optional, and you can adjust them to your personal preference and taste. The choices are almost endless. You can use nuts such as almond, cashew, pistachio and macadamia, or seeds such as hemp, sesame and pumpkin. Oats, coconut and rice are also popular, and milks made from potato are now also finding their way into grocery stores and local cafés.

In *Plant Milk Power*, we've assembled recipes for healthy everyday smoothies and vibrant, frosty fruit-based drinks that are perfect for summer. You'll find indulgent chocolate sweet treats as well as calming, relaxing and restorative hot drinks. And the collection wouldn't be complete without a section dedicated to plant milk cocktails and shakes that will bring all the vegans to the yard.

Have fun experimenting with different options, flavours and nutritional profiles ... there really is a plant-based milk to suit every palate and occasion!

Specialty Items You'll Need

Please check with a medical professional before including any adaptogens, supplements or herbal ingredients in your diet, especially if you are pregnant, breastfeeding, elderly or on medication.

Activated coconut charcoal powder

This powder binds to toxins in the body and removes them, relieving bloating and gas. While charcoal can be made from coal, wood or other materials, activated coconut charcoal powder is a superior food-grade product made from burning coconut shells at high heat. You should only use it occasionally and in very small doses.

Agar-agar

This clear, unflavoured thickening agent, or vegan-friendly 'gelatine' substitute, is made from red algae and used in many Asian-inspired desserts. Look for it online or in Asian grocery stores.

Ancho chilli powder

With its mild heat and delightful fruity flavour, the ancho chilli is one of the most commonly used chillies in Mexican cooking.

Ashwagandha powder

Often referred to as 'Indian ginseng', ashwagandha is an adaptogen used in Ayurvedic medicine as a nerve tonic that helps the body deal with stress and anxiety. It also helps contribute to a restful night's sleep.

Black tapioca pearls

Also known as boba, these are the 'bubbles' in bubble tea. They are chewy, sweet tapioca balls made from cassava root, which need to be cooked before eating. (Cook according to package instructions.) They can be white (translucent) or black, you can purchase them online or in Asian grocery stores, and they are becoming increasingly common in major supermarkets, too.

Boba straw

A large, wide straw capable of sucking up boba/tapioca pearls.

Ceremonial matcha

Matcha is the highest grade of Japanese green tea, and ceremonial matcha is the best-quality matcha available. It is the first pick of the tea leaves, and its chlorophyll-rich vibrant green hue, along with its delicate subtle flavour, denotes its high quality. Many recipes will recommend using cheap culinary-grade matcha but that is actually the lowest grade of matcha—it has a bitter aftertaste and yellowish green colour, and it needs loads of sugar to mask its lack of quality.

Dried blue butterfly pea flowers

Purchase these dried blue flowers (from the *Clitoria ternatea* plant) online, or in health-food or specialty tea stores. The tea has a subtle, lightly floral flavour and is caffeine free.

Introduction

Green and blue spirulina

These are types of algae that grow in both fresh and salt waters. They are considered to be a superfood due to their high content of vitamins, nutrients and protein, which make them powerful anti-inflammatories and antioxidants. Be sure to purchase organic spirulina only.

Maca powder

A Peruvian root vegetable belonging to the cruciferous family, maca has been used for centuries to increase stamina and endurance and boost energy. It has adaptogen qualities that may also improve mood and general cognitive function.

Medicinal mushroom powders

Mushrooms such as chaga, reishi, cordyceps and lion's mane have been used for centuries in traditional Chinese medicine. They are high in antioxidants and have a long list of health benefits, from increasing energy and stamina, to supporting the immune system and brain health. You can find mushroom powders at your local health-food store or online.

Nut milk bag

Made from nylon mesh or cotton, this bag is used to strain nut milk and separate it from the pulp, to create a smooth, silky nut milk.

Pashmak (Persian fairy floss)

Made from sugar, flour, oil and various flavourings that are finely spun into thin strands, Pashmak is found in gourmet food stores, online and in Middle Eastern grocery stores.

Introduction

Pashmak (Persian fairy floss)

Made from sugar, flour, oil and various flavourings that are finely spun into thin strands, Pashmak is found in gourmet food stores, online and in Middle Eastern grocery stores.

Peanut butter whiskey

Very popular in the USA and now available worldwide, peanut butter–flavoured whiskey is delicious if you like peanut butter flavours.

Sabja (sweet basil) seeds

These are found in Middle Eastern and Asian grocery stores or online, but you can substitute them with chia seeds, too.

Vegan collagen powder

This contains plant-based ingredients that build, boost and promote collagen production. Collagen-boosting supplements are available online and at health-food stores.

Vegan whipped cream

Ready-made vegan whipped cream is available at most supermarkets. If you can't find any in your area, substitute with whipped coconut cream.

Measurements Used In This Book

1 teaspoon = 5 ml

1 tablespoon = 20 ml (i.e. AU tablespoons, not US/UK/NZ)

1 cup = 250 ml/9 fl oz (i.e. metric cups, not US)

1 pint = 500 ml (i.e. US pints, not UK)

Basics

Nut And Seed Milk

Generally, you'll need to soak nuts and seeds in water prior to blending. Different seeds and nuts require different minimum soaking times, varying from 4 to 8 hours. As a basic rule, I prefer to soak them all overnight.

Soaking prior to blending not only softens the nuts, but also releases the nuts' enzyme inhibitors and phytic acid, which can interfere with our bodies' ability to absorb certain vitamins, minerals and other nutrients.

Make sure to discard the soaking water and use fresh filtered water to blend into nut milk.

1 cup nuts or seeds
3 cups (750 ml/1 ½ pints)
  filtered water

Optional add-ons

1-2 Medjool dates, pitted,
  or 1-2 teaspoons maple
  or agave syrup
1 pinch sea salt
½ teaspoon pure vanilla
  extract

Place the nuts (or seeds) into a fine-meshed sieve and rinse well. Place rinsed nuts into a bowl, cover with water and refrigerate for the minimum required time, or overnight.

Remove from the fridge, then drain and rinse well. Place the nuts into a high-speed blender with 3 cups (750 ml/1 ½ pints) filtered water and any add-ons (if using). Blitz for 1-2 minutes or until pureed, smooth and creamy.

Pour the blended milk into a nut milk bag or fine-meshed sieve lined with cheesecloth (muslin) set over a bowl. Strain the milk and set aside any remaining pulp.*

Store the milk in a glass container in the fridge for 3-5 days. The milk may separate while in the fridge—just shake before using.

Brazil nut milk: Use 1 ½ cups Brazil nuts to 3 cups (750 ml/1 ½ pints) filtered water.

Sesame seed milk: Use 1 ½ cups sesame seeds to 3 cups (750 ml/1 ½ pints) filtered water.

Minimum soaking times:
Brazil nuts and macadamias / 4 hours
Cashews and pecans / 6 hours
Almonds, hazelnuts, pistachios and
sesame seeds / 8 hours

Makes about 2 ½ cups (625ml) nut or seed milk

Not all nuts will have much remaining pulp once strained. Some, such as macadamia and cashew, are thick and creamy with just a little fine nut sediment but others, such as almond milk, have quite a bit of leftover pulp. To strain or not to strain is your choice; I always strain all nut milks for a finer texture. You can use leftover nut pulp in baked goods such as muffins, crackers or banana bread.

Soy Milk

Made from just two ingredients—dried soybeans and water—soy milk is an easy to make, nutritious plant-based drink. Compared with other plant-based milks, soy milk is higher in protein and lower in saturated fats.

Because you need to soak and cook the soybeans—you cannot consume raw soybeans—this recipe does have an extra step, but it's well worth it to have fresh soy milk at home. Making your own milk also allows you to add sweetener, salt or flavourings such as vanilla to your taste.

½ cup organic dried yellow soybeans
4 cups (1 litre/2 pints) filtered water

Optional add-ons

1-2 teaspoons maple or agave syrup (as desired)
1 pinch sea salt
½ teaspoon pure vanilla extract

Place the soybeans in a sieve and rinse well. Place rinsed soybeans into a container, cover with water and refrigerate for 10-12 hours or overnight.

Remove from the fridge, then drain and rinse well. Remove the skins from the soybeans and discard.

Place the soybeans into a high-speed blender with 4 cups (1 litre/2 pints) filtered water and blitz for 1-2 minutes until smooth, creamy and liquified.

Strain the soy mixture through a nut milk bag or fine-meshed sieve lined with cheesecloth (muslin) into a saucepan. Either keep or discard the pulp.*

Place the saucepan over medium heat and bring to the boil. Cook for 2-3 minutes, then reduce to a medium-low simmer. Simmer for about 15-20 minutes, stirring and skimming the foam that rises to the milk's surface.

Remove the milk from the heat. Add the maple or agave syrup, salt and vanilla extract (if using). You can drink the warm soy milk straight away, or allow to cool, pour into a glass container and store in the fridge for 3-4 days.

Makes about 3 cups (750 ml/1 ½ pints) soy milk.

Soy pulp is also known as okara. You can use it in stir-fries, vegetarian burgers, baked goods such as muffins, or smoothies. Keep refrigerated in a sealed container and use within 2-3 days.

Basics

Coconut And Oat Milk (No Soaking, No Cooking)

These are two of the easiest and quickest plant-based milks to make. They require no preparation, soaking or cooking. You can whip them up in your blender in seconds. Coconut milk and oat milk are super-quick, creamy, delicious and satisfying, and can be made at a moment's notice.

Oat Milk

Homemade oat milk is best served cold, because it has a tendency to thicken and become slimy when heated or overworked. The key to a light and tasty homemade oat milk is using ice-cold water and minimal processing (no nut milk bag required).

½ cup (50 g/1 ¾ oz) traditional rolled oats
3 cups (750 ml/1 ½ pints) ice-cold filtered water

Optional add-ons

1–2 teaspoons maple or agave syrup (as desired)
1 pinch sea salt
½ teaspoon pure vanilla extract

Place the oats and water into a high-speed blender and blitz for 20–30 seconds only. Do not over-process the oats.

Pour the mixture through a fine-meshed sieve into a bowl. Discard the pulp and rinse the sieve. If using any add-ons—such as sweetener, salt and/or vanilla —whisk through the milk. Strain the milk for a second time through a fine-meshed sieve, then store in a glass container in the fridge for 3–5 days. The milk may separate while in the fridge—just shake before using.

Makes about 2 ½ cups (625 ml/1 ⅓ pints) oat milk.

Coconut Milk

Thick, creamy, rich and so simple to make, coconut milk is one of my favourite plant-based milks. It has a distinct coconut taste and is delicious when paired with chocolate and tropical fruits.

2 cups (130 g/4 ½ oz) coconut flakes
3 cups (750 ml/1 ½ pints) cold filtered water

Place the coconut flakes and water into a high-speed blender.

Blitz until well combined, then strain through a nut milk bag into a clean glass container. Store container in the fridge for 3-5 days. The milk may separate while in the fridge—just shake before using.

Makes about 3 cups (750 ml/1 ½ pints) coconut milk.

Rice Milk

There are two different methods for making rice milk, depending on the creaminess and texture you prefer. You can either cook and cool the rice before blending, or you can soak raw rice grains then blend. You can add sweeteners, salt or vanilla if you wish, just taste and adjust to your preferences.

Cooked Rice Method

Using cooked rice yields a slightly creamier, denser texture, and is a convenient way to use any leftover cooked rice.

1 cup (210 g/7 ½ oz) white or brown basmati rice, cooked and cooled
3 cups (750 ml/1 ½ pints) filtered water

Optional add-ons

1-2 Medjool dates, pitted, or 1-2 teaspoons maple or agave syrup
1 pinch sea salt
½ teaspoon pure vanilla extract

Place the rice into a high-speed blender with the water and any add-ons (if using). Blitz for about 1-2 minutes, or until pureed, smooth and creamy. There is no need to strain this milk. Store the rice milk in a glass container in the fridge for 3-5 days. The milk may separate while in the fridge—just shake before using.

Makes about 3 ½ cups (875 ml/1 ¾ pints).

Raw Rice Method

You need to soak raw rice to soften it before blending. Rice milk made from raw rice creates a milk with a finer, slightly thinner texture.

1 cup (200 g/7 oz) white or brown basmati rice, raw
3 cups (750 ml/1 ½ pints) filtered water

Optional add-ons

1-2 Medjool dates, pitted, or 1-2 teaspoons maple or agave syrup
1 pinch sea salt
½ teaspoon pure vanilla extract

Place the rice into a fine-meshed sieve and rinse very well. Place into a container, cover with water and refrigerate overnight.

Remove from the fridge, then drain and rinse well. Place the rice into a high-speed blender with 3 cups (750 ml/1 ½ pints) filtered water and any add-ons (if using). Blitz for 1-2 minutes, or until pureed, smooth and creamy. There is no need to strain this milk.

Store the rice milk in a glass container in the fridge for 3-5 days. The milk may separate while in the fridge—just shake before using.

Makes about 3 ½ cups (875ml) raw rice milk

Basics

Potato Milk

The newest kid on the plant-based milk block is potato milk, and it already has a devout following. It's the most sustainable plant milk to make, as potatoes need the least amount of resources to grow compared with almonds, oats and even soybeans. It has a creamy, milky and mild taste, which makes it great for smoothies. Potatoes must be cooked prior to blending. The added ground almonds create a creamier texture, and the added sweetener, salt and vanilla really enhance the taste and flavour of this milk. This milk doesn't require straining, because it's very creamy and emulsified, but you can strain it for a finer texture if you wish.

1 russet potato, peeled, (about 250 g/9 oz)
2 tablespoons ground almonds
4 cups (1 litre/2 pints) filtered water
2-3 Medjool dates, pitted, or 1-2 teaspoons maple or agave syrup (as desired)
1 good pinch sea salt
½ teaspoon pure vanilla extract

Cut the peeled potato into 5-cm (2-inch) cubes. Place into a saucepan, cover with water, and bring to the boil. Cook for about 9–10 minutes or until cooked through—they should be soft and tender, but not falling apart. Remove from the stove, then drain and rinse with cold water. Place into a high-speed blender with the ground almonds, 4 cups (1 litre/2 pints) filtered water, dates, sea salt and vanilla extract.

Blitz until smooth, creamy and liquified, about 2 minutes. Taste and adjust seasoning as desired.

If straining, pour the blended mixture into a nut milk bag or fine-meshed sieve lined with cheesecloth (muslin) set over a bowl. Strain the milk and discard the solids. Store the potato milk in a glass container in the fridge for up to 3 days. The milk may separate while in the fridge—just shake before using.

Makes about 4 ½ cups (1.125 litres/2 ¼ pints).

Cold

Iced Matcha Latte

Nutty and sweet, homemade pistachio milk is the perfect complement to the clean and lightly grassy flavours of ceremonial matcha (green tea powder). Poured over ice and topped with a decadent dollop of matcha whipped cream, this latte is refreshingly cool.

2 teaspoons organic ceremonial matcha
90 ml (3 fl oz) water, just boiled
1–2 teaspoons agave syrup (optional)
Ice cubes
1 cup (250 ml/9 fl oz) pistachio milk

Whipped coconut cream

¼ cup (60 ml/2 fl oz) chilled coconut cream**
½ teaspoon organic ceremonial matcha
1 teaspoon powdered sugar

Topping

Extra matcha

Sift the matcha into a small bowl, pour in 2 tablespoons (40 ml/1 ½ fl oz) just-boiled water and whisk* until a smooth paste forms. Add the remaining water and whisk until fully blended and frothy. Add the agave syrup (if using) and give it another whisk, then place in the fridge and chill for about 15–20 minutes.

Just before you're ready to serve your iced matcha, make the whipped cream.

Place the chilled coconut cream into a bowl. Sift over the matcha and powdered sugar, then whisk vigorously until light, whipped and creamy.

Place the ice cubes into a glass. Pour over the pistachio milk, then the chilled matcha. Top with a dollop of whipped coconut cream, dust with a little extra matcha and enjoy.

*You can use a traditional matcha whisk, known as a chasen, or a small hand-held milk frother. If using a milk frother, pour all the water over the matcha powder and blend until combined.

**Keep a can of coconut cream in the fridge so it's well chilled and ready to use. Scoop off the thick, creamy top to mix into this rich tropical drink. You can use the remaining, thinner milk in smoothies.

Cold

Strawberry Milk

When life gives you strawberries, make strawberry milk! This isn't the strawberry milk you had when you were a kid—it's so much better!

The combination of fresh, ripe, juicy strawberries, vanilla bean paste and creamy Brazil nut milk makes a sweet, rich, berry-flavoured pink drink, which tastes as good as it looks. Easy to make with just a few ingredients, this will soon become one of your favourite new blends.

1 ¼ cups (310 ml/10 ½ fl oz) Brazil nut milk
1 cup (180 g/6 ¼ oz) ripe fresh strawberries, hulled
1 Medjool date, pitted, or 1-2 teaspoons maple or agave syrup
¼ teaspoon vanilla bean paste
1 pinch sea salt

Place the Brazil nut milk, strawberries, date (or syrup if using), vanilla bean paste and sea salt into a high-speed blender and blitz until smooth. Place strawberry milk into a glass container and refrigerate until chilled, or pour into an ice-filled glass and enjoy immediately.

Keeps in the fridge for 3 days.

Orange Creamsicle

Creamy, sweet and chilled, the orange creamsicle is a classic pairing of citrusy orange and heady vanilla bean, reminiscent of those vanilla ice-cream popsicles wrapped in icy fruit juice you used to eat as a kid. This plant milk smoothie uses creamy, buttery macadamia milk with the unexpected addition of juicy mango for a tropical twist. It tastes like a lazy summer's day.

½ cup (125 ml/4 fl oz) macadamia milk
½ frozen banana, diced
⅓ cup (80 ml/2 ½ fl oz) vegan vanilla yoghurt (or silken tofu)
1 orange (about 180 g/ 6 ¼ oz), peeled and diced then frozen
60 g (2 oz) diced frozen mango
½ teaspoon pure vanilla extract
1 teaspoon orange zest

Toppings
Vegan whipped cream
Fresh orange zest
Fresh orange slice

Place all the ingredients into a high-speed blender and blitz until smooth and creamy.

Pour into a tall, chilled glass, then top with a little whipped cream, fresh orange zest and a round slice of fresh orange on the side.

Cold

Red Velvet

The toasty, nutty flavours of hazelnut milk complement the chocolatey raw cacao powder and earthy beetroot in this smoothie. The frozen berries add a load of antioxidant goodness, as well as a subtle sweet-tart flavour that rounds out the richness of the other ingredients.

1 cup (250 ml/9 fl oz) hazelnut milk
1 cup (140 g/5 oz) frozen mixed berries (strawberries, blackberries and raspberries)
½ frozen banana, diced
⅓ small raw red beetroot (about 50 g/1 ¾ oz), diced
3 Medjool dates, pitted
2 tablespoons raw cacao powder
¾ teaspoon pure vanilla extract

Toppings
Mixed berries
Cacao nibs
Raw cacao powder

Place all the ingredients into a high-speed blender and blitz for 1–2 minutes, or until frosty, smooth and creamy.

Pour into a tall, chilled glass and top with some more mixed berries, cacao nibs and a dusting of cacao powder to serve.

Cold

Ultimate Chocolate Milkshake

Nostalgic for an old-fashioned chocolate milkshake? This plant milk version—with creamy, toasty hazelnut milk and chocolate sorbet—is a vegan-friendly take on the classic milkshake. It's laden with rich, deep, creamy chocolate flavours, using instant espresso powder and vanilla extract to highlight the chocolatey notes.

½ cup (125 ml/4 fl oz) hazelnut milk

1 cup (250 ml/9 fl oz) chocolate sorbet, slightly softened

1 teaspoon instant espresso powder

½ teaspoon pure vanilla extract

2 tablespoons Chocolate Syrup (see That's How the Cookie Crumbles recipe, page 58) or hazelnut spread

Toppings

1 scoop (55 g/2 oz) chocolate sorbet

Vegan whipped cream

Vegan chocolate sprinkles

Vegan dark chocolate curls

Vegan chocolate-dipped wafer roll

Maraschino cherry

Place the hazelnut milk, chocolate sorbet, espresso powder and vanilla extract into a high-speed blender, then blitz until smooth, frosty and creamy. Spoon the chocolate syrup (or hazelnut spread if using) into the bottom of a chilled, tall glass and pour over the chocolate milkshake. Top with a scoop of chocolate sorbet, a ribbon of whipped cream, and some chocolate sprinkles and dark chocolate curls. Place a chocolate-dipped wafer roll and maraschino cherry on top to serve.

Cold

Indian Summer

Lassis are yoghurt-based, lightly spiced drinks that originated in India. Thirst-quenching, cooling and refreshing, they are popular everywhere. And with good reason—they are healthy and delicious.

This recipe combines ripe, lightly perfumed sweet mangos, creamy coconut yoghurt and lush cashew milk. The ground turmeric adds a boost of antioxidants, and a little black pepper helps activate its full healing potential.

⅓ cup (80 ml/2 ½ fl oz) cashew milk
1 cup (150 g/5 ½ oz) diced frozen mango
⅔ cup (160 ml/5 ¼ fl oz) coconut yoghurt
3 teaspoons coconut sugar
½ teaspoon pure vanilla extract
½ teaspoon ground cardamom
¼ teaspoon ground turmeric
1 good pinch freshly ground black pepper
Squeeze of lime juice
Ice cubes

Toppings

Flaked coconut
Pistachio slivers
Calendula petals

Add all the ingredients into a high-speed blender and blitz until pureed and smooth. Pour over a tall glass filled with ice cubes, and top with flaked coconut, pistachio slivers and calendula petals to garnish.

The Ripe Cherry

Chock-a-block with coconut and dark chocolate, and bursting with sweet-tart cherries, this coconut milk-based milkshake is a rich, decadent treat. It tastes just like your favourite coconut and cherry chocolate bar, only vegan and in a glass.

½ cup (125 ml/4 fl oz) coconut milk

1 cup (150 g/5 ½ oz) frozen cherries

1 cup (250 ml/9 fl oz) vegan coconut ice cream

30 g (1 oz) coconut vegan chocolate bar, roughly chopped

2-3 tablespoons Chocolate Syrup (see That's How the Cookie Crumbles recipe, page 58), as desired

Toppings

Vegan whipped cream
Flaked or shredded coconut
Vegan dark chocolate chunks
Extra Chocolate Syrup, to drizzle
Fresh cherries

Add the coconut milk, cherries and coconut ice cream into a high-speed blender. Blitz for 30-40 seconds until smooth and creamy. If you'd like a thinner milkshake, add a little more milk and blend again. Add the chopped chocolate bar and blitz quickly for 5-10 seconds until just crumbled.

Spoon the chocolate syrup into the bottom of a tall glass, then pour in the milkshake.

Top with whipped cream, flaked coconut and dark chocolate chunks. Drizzle over a little chocolate syrup and top with a fresh cherry or two.

Blue Butterfly Bubble Tea

Bubble tea with sweet, chewy tapioca pearls is so fun to eat and drink that it's achieved global cult status. This recipe combines beautiful blue butterfly bubble tea with homemade oat milk for a vegan twist on the classic drink. For a little tropical flavour, try using coconut milk instead of oat milk.

½ cup (125 ml/4 fl oz) boiling water
1 ½ tablespoons dried blue butterfly pea flowers
¼ teaspoon pure vanilla extract
Ice cubes
⅓ cup (80 ml/2 ½ fl oz) cold oat milk
½ cup (85 g/3 oz) black tapioca pearls (black sugar boba), cooked according to package instructions

Brown Sugar Syrup

¼ cup (55 g/2 oz) brown sugar
2 tablespoons water

To make the tea, pour the boiling water over the dried blue butterfly pea flowers and let steep for 10 minutes. Strain the tea into a glass container, stir through the vanilla extract, and refrigerate until chilled and ready to use.

To make the brown sugar syrup, combine the sugar and water in a small pot over high heat and bring to the boil. Continue boiling for about 1 ½ to 2 minutes, or until the liquid has reduced and thickened. Remove from the heat, add the cooked, drained tapioca pearls and combine, completely covering the pearls in the syrup. Place in the refrigerator and chill for 10-15 minutes.

To assemble, spoon the tapioca pearls into the bottom of a tall glass and top with ice cubes. Pour in the chilled oat milk, then pour over the blue butterfly tea. Serve with a thick boba straw and enjoy.

Cold

Horchata

This vegan take on the classic Mexican horchata is lightly spiced and refreshing. Homemade rice milk and almond milk, combined with a generous amount of both cinnamon and vanilla, make this drink really special. You can also make this horchata with coconut milk.

1 cup (250 ml/9 fl oz) rice milk
½ cup (125 ml/4 fl oz) almond milk
1 tablespoon vegan condensed coconut milk or agave syrup
½ teaspoon ground cinnamon
¼–½ teaspoon vanilla bean paste or extract (as desired)
Ice cubes

Toppings
Toasted flaked almonds
Ground cinnamon
1 cinnamon stick

Place the rice milk, almond milk, condensed coconut milk or agave syrup, ground cinnamon and vanilla bean paste into a high-speed blender, then blitz until frothy.

Pour into a large glass filled with ice, then top with a sprinkle of toasted flaked almonds and a little ground cinnamon. Serve with a cinnamon stick.

Pistachio Rose Lassi

Cooling, refreshing and exotic, this blend of pistachio milk, coconut yoghurt and rosewater is perfect on a hot summer's day. Homemade pistachio milk has a distinctive yet subtle flavour and combines perfectly with the floral rosewater and sweet, citrusy cardamom. Make a batch or two, and chill well in the fridge or pour over ice for an immediate thirst-quencher.

⅔-1 cup (160-250 ml/
   5 ¼ -9 fl oz) cold
   pistachio milk
1 cup (250 ml/9 fl oz)
   coconut yoghurt
2 Medjool dates, pitted
1 ½ teaspoons rosewater
1 teaspoon organic
   ceremonial matcha
¼ teaspoon vanilla bean
   paste
¼ teaspoon ground
   cardamom, or seeds from
   8 green cardamom pods
1 small nob fresh ginger,
   about thumbnail size
   (optional)
1 tiny pinch sea salt

Toppings

Rose or pistachio-
   flavoured pashmak
   (Persian fairy floss)
Organic edible rose petals
Pistachio slivers

Place all the ingredients into a high-speed blender and blitz for 30-40 seconds, or until smooth, frosty and creamy. Serve chilled or pour into a tall glass filled with ice. Top with a little pashmak and a sprinkle of rose petals and pistachio slivers.

Cold

Rose Falooda

2 tablespoons Rose Syrup
¼ cup soaked
  vermicelli, drained
¼ cup (60 ml/2 fl oz) cubed
  Rose Jelly (or any red
  vegan jelly), or 1 piece
  Turkish delight, sliced
2 teaspoons sabja seeds,
  soaked in boiling water
  for 30 minutes, drained
½–⅔ cup (125–160 ml/
  4–5 ¼ fl oz) cashew milk
1 scoop (55 g/2 oz) vegan
  vanilla ice cream

Rose Syrup

½ cup (125 ml/4 fl oz)
  water
½ cup (110 g/3 ¾ oz)
  caster (granulated) sugar
2 teaspoons rosewater
2 drops pink food
  colouring
¼ teaspoon pure vanilla
  extract (optional)

Rose Jelly

1 cup (250 ml/9 fl oz)
  water
¼ cup caster (granulated)
  sugar
2 teaspoons rosewater
1–2 drops red food
  colouring
1 ½ teaspoons agar-agar
  powder

Syrupy sweet rose-infused milk dances happily with vivid pink jelly, slippery vermicelli and gelatinous sabja (sweet basil) seeds in this beautiful ice-cream float. Rose falooda has its origins in Persia, but has travelled across many countries and cultures with each making its mark. I've added some different ingredients to make this playful beauty a vegan-friendly treat, starring lush cashew milk.

If you can't find sabja seeds, you can replace them with chia seeds for a similar effect. If you're short on time, you can replace the rose jelly with store-bought vegan raspberry jelly or even cubed Turkish delight for a super-sweet treat.

To make the rose syrup, place the water and sugar in a small saucepan over medium–high heat and bring to the boil. Cook for 3–4 minutes until the sugar has dissolved and the mixture has thickened slightly. Remove from the heat and whisk in the rosewater, food colouring and vanilla extract (if using). Allow to cool, then store in a sealed glass jar in the fridge for up to 2 weeks. Makes ½ cup (125 ml/4 fl oz).

To make the rose jelly, place the water, sugar, rosewater, red food colouring and agar-agar into a saucepan. Place over medium–high heat, whisk to combine and bring to the boil. Boil for about 3–4 minutes, or until the sugar and agar-agar have completely dissolved. Remove from the heat, pour into a shallow heatproof container and allow to cool. Place in the fridge to set for an hour. Once cooled, dice into cubes. Keep covered in the fridge for 5–7 days.

Toppings

Organic edible rose petals
Pistachio slivers
Rose pashmak (Persian
  fairy floss)

To assemble the falooda, place the rose syrup into the bottom of a large, tall glass. Then add the vermicelli, jelly and soaked sabja seeds. Pour over the cashew milk and top with a scoop of ice cream. Sprinkle over the dried rose petals and pistachios, and top with a little pashmak. Serve with a spoon and thick straw.

47

Cold

Wild Thing

Don't underestimate the mighty power of these little purple fruits. Wild blueberries and açai berries are superfood rock stars, and shine brightly in this intensely vibrant purple smoothie.

Bursting with intense, juicy and sweet berry flavour, plus creamy cashew milk rounded out with a spoonful of lush cashew butter, this will become one of your all-time favourite smoothies.

1 ¼ cups (310 ml/10 ½ fl oz) cashew milk
1 cup (140 g/5 oz) frozen wild blueberries
100 g (3 ½ oz) frozen açai fruit puree
1 frozen banana, diced
3 Medjool dates, pitted
1 tablespoon cashew butter
1 tablespoon hemp seeds
1 teaspoon freshly grated ginger
½ teaspoon pure vanilla extract
1 pinch sea salt
1 scoop vegan protein powder (optional)

Toppings

Fresh berries
Chopped cashews

Place all the ingredients into a high-speed blender and blitz until smooth and creamy. If you like a thinner smoothie, add a little more cashew milk.

Pour into a tall, chilled glass and top with a few fresh berries and a sprinkle of chopped cashews.

The Pink Dragon

Dragon fruit, or pitaya, is native to Mexico and Central America but grows in tropical regions around the world. This fruit comes in three different colours, but the vibrant pink is my favourite. It's loaded with prebiotic fibre, antioxidants and vitamin C. Blend it up with protein-rich cashew milk, silken tofu and chia seeds for a tasty, and seriously healthy, start to your day.

1 cup (250 ml/9 fl oz) cashew milk
½ cup (75 g/2 ½ oz) frozen pitted cherries
½ cup (70 g/2 ½ oz) frozen raspberries
½ frozen banana, diced
100 g (3 ½ oz) frozen dragon fruit (pitaya) pulp
100 g (3 ½ oz) organic silken tofu
3 Medjool dates, pitted
20 g (¾ oz) shredded coconut
3 teaspoons chia seeds

Toppings

Fresh pink and white dragon fruit pieces
Fresh cherries
Fresh raspberries
Shredded coconut

Place the cashew milk, cherries, raspberries, banana, dragon fruit, tofu, dates and coconut into a high-speed blender and blitz until smooth and frosty. Pour into a large, chilled glass and stir through the chia seeds. Top with fresh dragon fruit pieces, cherries and raspberries, and sprinkle over a little shredded coconut to serve.

Cold

Left: Wild
Thing

Right: The
Pink Dragon

Cold

50

Cold

PB & J

Every kid's favourite flavour combination comes together in this delicious two-toned drink. Creamy peanut butter is infused with rich almond milk and fresh strawberry chia jam—no white bread required! This smoothie is packed with protein, rich in fibre and has plenty of omega-3 fatty acids for good health. Top with a fresh strawberry, peanut butter and a sprinkle of chopped, salted and roasted peanuts.

1 cup (250 ml/9 fl oz) almond milk
1 frozen banana, diced
2 ½ tablespoons peanut butter
2 Medjool dates, pitted
1 ½ teaspoons linseed (flax seeds)
1 pinch sea salt
2 ice cubes

Strawberry Chia Jam

150 g (5 ½ oz) fresh, ripe strawberries, chopped
2 teaspoons chia seeds
2 teaspoons maple syrup

Toppings

Peanut butter
Salted roasted peanuts, chopped
1 fresh strawberry

To make the chia jam, place the chopped strawberries, chia seeds and maple syrup into a bowl and mash together, combining well. Set aside for about 30-40 minutes, or until the chia seeds have absorbed the liquid and the mixture is jam-like.

To make the smoothie, place the almond milk, banana, peanut butter, dates, linseed, salt and ice cubes into a high-speed blender, then blitz to combine until smooth and creamy, as desired.

Spoon the chia jam into the bottom and around the sides of a chilled glass, and pour over the peanut butter smoothie. Top with a dollop of peanut butter, some chopped roasted peanuts, and a strawberry on the side. Serve with a spoon and thick straw.

Cold

The Game-Changer

Thick and creamy, frosty and cold, this smoothie is filled with loads of healthy vegetables and good fats, yet tastes like mint chocolate-chip ice cream. Now, I know what you're thinking: 'Cauliflower in a smoothie? Are you kidding me? That can't be right!' But you can't taste it, I promise! Frozen cauliflower adds a thick, creamy texture to your smoothie without the cauliflower taste. It's a game-changer when you're trying to add more veggies into your diet.

1 ¼ cup (310 ml/10 ½ fl oz) oat milk
1 cup (30 g/1 oz) loosely packed baby spinach
½ cup (45 g/1 ½ oz) frozen riced cauliflower
½ frozen banana, diced
¼ frozen avocado
10–12 fresh mint leaves (as desired)
2 Medjool dates, pitted
½ teaspoon pure vanilla extract
¼ teaspoon wheat grass powder
⅓ cup ice cubes
1 tablespoon vegan chocolate chips or cacao nibs

Toppings

Coconut whipped cream
Fresh mint leaves
Extra vegan chocolate chips or cacao nibs
Raw cacao powder

Place all the ingredients except the chocolate chips (or cacao nibs if using) into a high-speed blender, then blitz until smooth and creamy. Taste, adding a little more mint or vanilla if desired, and some more oat milk if the smoothie is too thick for your liking.

Pour the smoothie into a tall, chilled glass and garnish with a dollop of coconut whipped cream, some fresh mint leaves, a few chocolate chips (or cacao nibs) and a dusting of cacao powder.

Peachy Keen

Sweet peaches team up with toasty, nutty walnut milk in this creamy and lightly spiced breakfast smoothie. With a pinch of warming cinnamon, the crunchy toasted-oat topping has this smoothie tasting like your favourite peach crumble dessert.

⅓ cup (80 ml/2 ½ fl oz) walnut milk
2 cups (350 g/12 oz) fresh or frozen peaches (or canned peaches in natural peach juice)
¼ cup (60 ml/2 fl oz) peach nectar
1 tablespoon traditional rolled oats
1 tablespoon almond butter
1 tablespoon maple syrup
⅛ teaspoon ground cinnamon

Toasted Cinnamon Oat Crumble

½ cup (50 g/1 ¾ oz) traditional whole rolled oats
¼ cup (30 g/1 oz) flaked almonds
2 tablespoons shredded coconut
2 tablespoons maple syrup
2 teaspoons melted coconut oil
½ teaspoon ground cinnamon or pumpkin-pie spice mix

To make the toasted cinnamon oat crumble, add all the crumble ingredients into a small bowl. Toss together and place on a baking sheet. Bake in a preheated oven at 180°C (350°F) for about 15 minutes, or until golden and lightly toasted. Cool and store in an airtight container, where it will keep for 2 weeks. Makes about 1 cup (90 g/3 oz).

To make the smoothie, place all the smoothie ingredients into a high-speed blender, then blitz until smooth and creamy. Pour into a chilled glass and sprinkle over a little toasted cinnamon oat crumble to serve.

Cold

Carrot Cake

Warming spices, earthy sweet carrots and toasted nutty pecans—all the flavours of carrot cake are packed in this delicious, healthy and 'good for you' smoothie. It tastes just like a carrot cake served chilled in a tall glass. The star here is pecan milk, but you could swap it out for walnut milk if you prefer. Both milks work equally well in this smoothie that's perfect for breakfast or an afternoon treat.

1 cup (250 ml/9 fl oz) pecan milk
1 frozen banana, diced
1 cup (100 g/3 ½ oz) grated carrot
½ cup (80 g/2 ¾ oz) diced frozen pineapple
2 Medjool dates, pitted
3 teaspoons fresh lemon juice
1 teaspoon freshly grated ginger
½ teaspoon pure vanilla extract
½ teaspoon ground cinnamon
1 small pinch ground cloves
1 small pinch freshly grated nutmeg
3–4 ice cubes

Toppings
Toasted chopped pecans
Toasted coconut flakes
Carrot curls

Place the pecan milk, banana, grated carrot, pineapple, dates, lemon juice, ginger, vanilla extract and spices into a high-speed blender and blitz until smooth. Add a few ice cubes and blend again until creamy and frosty. Taste and adjust the flavours, adding a little more spice if desired. Pour into a tall glass and top with a sprinkle of toasted chopped pecans, toasted coconut flakes and carrot curls.

Cold

That's How The Cookie Crumbles

Chocolate cookies, rich French vanilla ice cream, creamy oat milk and a dash of pure vanilla really elevate this super-thick milkshake to super-star status.

½ cup (125 ml/4 fl oz) oat milk
1 ½ cups (375 ml/12 ½ fl oz) vegan French vanilla ice cream
¼ teaspoon pure vanilla extract
3 Oreo cookies (crème-filled vegan chocolate sandwich cookies)

Chocolate Syrup

⅔ cup (150 g/5 ½ oz) caster (granulated) sugar
½ cup (55 g/2 oz) raw cacao powder
½ cup (125 ml/4 fl oz) water
½ teaspoon pure vanilla extract
1 pinch sea salt

Toppings

2 teaspoons Chocolate Syrup
3 extra Oreo cookies (2 whole, 1 crushed)
Vegan whipped cream
Vegan dark chocolate shavings

To make the chocolate syrup, sift the sugar and cacao powder into a small saucepan and add the water. Place over medium heat and whisk together. Continue whisking as the mixture cooks for 4–5 minutes, or until thick and syrupy. Remove from the heat and whisk in the vanilla extract and sea salt. Cool at room temperature, then store in a sealed container in the fridge for up to 2 weeks. Makes about 1 cup (250 ml/9 fl oz).

To make the milkshake, place the oat milk, ice cream, vanilla extract and one cookie into a high-speed blender, then blitz until smooth and creamy. Add the remaining two cookies and pulse until just broken with chunky cookie crumbs visible.

Drizzle the chocolate syrup around the inside of a tall, chilled soda fountain glass and pour in the milkshake. Sprinkle over half the extra cookie crumbs, then top with a lush ribbon of whipped cream. Garnish with the two whole cookies, a final sprinkle of the remaining cookie crumbs and a few dark chocolate shavings. Serve with a tall milkshake spoon and thick straw.

The Mermaid

Layered waves of blue and green swirl together in this super-rich antioxidant smoothie. Chia seeds, coconut yoghurt and banana smoothie are infused with vivid hues from spirulina, an aquatic superfood. Good for you and beautiful, too, this magical smoothie will have you feeling like a happy little mermaid splashing about in a tropical lagoon.

Chia Seed Layer

½ cup (125 ml/4 fl oz) coconut milk
1 tablespoon chia seeds
1 teaspoon agave syrup
¼ teaspoon green spirulina

Coconut Yoghurt Layer

½ cup (125 ml/4 fl oz) coconut yoghurt
1 teaspoon agave syrup
½ teaspoon blue spirulina

Banana Smoothie Layer

½ frozen banana, diced
½ cup (80 g/2 ¾ oz) diced frozen pineapple
⅓ cup (80 ml/2 ½ fl oz) coconut milk
¼ teaspoon green spirulina

Topping

Coconut flakes

To make the chia seed layer, combine all the ingredients in a small bowl and stir well to combine. Refrigerate for 1–2 hours or overnight, until the chia seeds have absorbed all the coconut milk and are plump.

To make the coconut yoghurt layer, whisk all the ingredients together. Refrigerate until required.

To make the banana smoothie layer, place all the ingredients into a high-speed blender and blitz until smooth, frosty and well combined.

Assemble the mermaid smoothie by placing the chia seed mixture in the bottom of a tall glass. Top with a layer of blue coconut yoghurt, then pour the banana smoothie over the top. Sprinkle over a few coconut flakes, serve with a straw and spoon, and enjoy.

Cold

Super Green Monster

Kid tested and approved, this smoothie is fully loaded with all the good green stuff—spinach, zucchini and spirulina—while the banana and pineapple bring plenty of fibre and sweet tropical flavours. Creamy almond milk and avocado bring it all together with a touch of good heart-healthy fats. You won't believe drinking your veggies can taste so good. You might just turn into the Incredible Hulk after drinking it!

1-1 ¼ cups (250-310 ml/ 9-10 ½ fl oz) almond milk (as desired)

1 cup (30 g/1 oz) loosely packed baby spinach

1 cup (80 g/2 ¾ oz) diced frozen pineapple

⅓ cup (50 g/1 ¾ oz) chopped zucchini

1 kiwifruit (100 g/3 ½ oz), peeled

1 frozen banana, diced

1 Medjool date, pitted

½ small avocado (50 g/ 1 ¾ oz)

1 teaspoon spirulina

Toppings
Pineapple wedge
Kiwifruit slices

Place all the ingredients into a high-speed blender and blitz for 1-2 minutes, or until smooth and creamy. Pour into a tall, chilled glass and garnish with a pineapple wedge and kiwifruit slices.

Cold

Coachella Tahini Date Shake

Palm Springs and the Coachella Valley in California have been shaking date shakes since 1928, long before the rock-star A-listers and boho beauties arrived in town.

This healthier version of the famous Palm Springs date shake omits the ice cream, adding a halva-like flavour with nutty sesame seed milk, rich tahini, caramel-flavoured dates and a hit of spicy cinnamon. Protein-fuelled hemp seeds and stamina-enhancing maca will keep you dancing all night long.

1 cup (250 ml/9 fl oz)
  sesame seed milk
⅔ cup ice cubes
½ frozen banana, diced
4 Medjool dates, pitted
2 tablespoons tahini paste
1 tablespoon hemp seeds
1 teaspoon maca powder
¼ teaspoon ground
  cinnamon
1 pinch sea salt

Toppings

Ground cinnamon
Toasted sesame seeds
Hemp seeds
Dried orange slice
Tahini

Place all the shake ingredients into a high-speed blender and blitz for 1–1 ½ minutes, or until smooth and frosty. Pour into a tall, chilled glass and top with sprinkles of cinnamon, sesame seeds and hemp seeds. Garnish with a slice of dried orange and a drizzle of tahini.

Ultimate Chai Latte

Traditional Indian chai is a heady fusion of spiced black tea and sweetened cows' milk. I prefer this vegan version using soy milk.

The flavour and texture of homemade soy milk blends beautifully with the aromatic chai spices. This warming drink is perfect with breakfast or as an afternoon pick-me-up.

3 tablespoons Chai Mix
¼ cup (60 ml/2 fl oz) water
1 cup (250 ml/9 fl oz) soy milk

Chai Mix

30 whole green cardamom pods
10 whole cloves
6 whole star anise
4 cinnamon sticks
1 ¾ teaspoons whole black peppercorns
½ teaspoon freshly grated nutmeg
70 g (2 ½ oz) freshly grated ginger
1 cup (80 g/2 ¾ oz) loose-leaf black Assam tea
½ cup (125 ml/4 fl oz) agave syrup, warmed

Toppings

Ground cinnamon
Frothed soy milk or coconut cream

To make the chai mix: Roughly crush the cardamom, cloves, star anise, cinnamon and peppercorns into small pieces using either a mortar and pestle or spice grinder. Crushing the spices allows more flavour to be released while brewing, but don't get carried away here. Take care not to pulverise the spice mixture, which would result in a gritty, powdery brew.

Now, combine the crushed spices with the nutmeg, ginger, tea leaves and warmed agave syrup, mixing well. Store the chai mix in an airtight glass container in the fridge until ready to brew. It keeps for about 3 weeks. Makes about 2 cups (360 g/12 ½ oz) or 8 serves.

To brew the chai: Place 3 heaped tablespoons of the chai mixture into a small pot. Add ¼ cup (60 ml/2 fl oz) water and 1 cup (250 ml/9 fl oz) soy milk, or for a milkier tea, omit the water and use 1 ¼ cups (310 ml/10 ½ fl oz) soy milk. Simmer over low-medium heat for about 4-5 minutes until hot. Remove from the heat and steep for a further 4-5 minutes.

Strain the warmed chai into a glass or mug. Taste and add more agave if desired. Top with extra frothed milk or a dollop of coconut cream, and dust with a sprinkle of ground cinnamon.

Hot

The Wake-Up Call

The matcha latte has gone rogue—all your caffeinated dreams come true in this two-toned morning wake-up call. The pistachio milk blends beautifully with the grassy ceremonial matcha flavours, and it's topped with a second hit of caffeine in the guise of a glossy, fluffy, creamy, dreamy, whipped dalgona coffee.

1 ½ teaspoons organic ceremonial matcha powder
⅓ cup (80 ml/2 ½ fl oz) water, just boiled
⅔ cup (160 ml/5 ¼ fl oz) pistachio milk, warmed
2 teaspoons Vanilla Syrup

Vanilla Syrup

½ cup (125 ml/4 fl oz) water
½ cup (120 g/4 oz) caster (granulated) sugar
½ teaspoon pure vanilla extract

Whipped Coffee

2 tablespoons instant espresso coffee
2 tablespoons caster (granulated) sugar
2 tablespoons hot water

To make the vanilla syrup, combine the water and sugar in a small pot over high heat. Bring to the boil, whisking the sugar until dissolved, and let the mixture bubble away for 4–5 minutes until slightly reduced and syrupy. Remove from the heat, whisk in the vanilla extract, and cool to room temperature. Keeps in a sealed container in the fridge for 2–3 weeks.

To make the whipped coffee, place all the ingredients into a small bowl and whisk using an electric hand-mixer. Beat for 3–5 minutes, or until the texture is glossy, smooth and firm enough to hold creamy peaks.

Sift the matcha powder into a small bowl using a fine-meshed sieve. Add 2 tablespoons just-boiled water to the matcha and whisk* until a smooth paste forms. Add the remaining water and whisk again until fully blended and frothy.

Pour the warmed pistachio milk into a glass, stir in the vanilla syrup, and pour over the matcha. Serve topped with spoonfuls of whipped coffee.

You can use a traditional matcha whisk, known as a chasen, or a small hand-held milk frother. If using a milk frother, pour all the water onto the matcha powder and blend until combined.

Toasted Coconut Golden Latte

Golden lattes are lightly spiced milk drinks laced with turmeric, ginger and black pepper, to name some of the warming spices. Soothing and comforting, with anti-inflammatory benefits from the ground turmeric, golden milk or turmeric lattes are used in traditional Ayurvedic medicine.

1 ⅓ cups (330 ml/11 fl oz) Toasted Coconut Milk
2 teaspoons maple or agave syrup (as desired)
1 teaspoon extra virgin coconut oil
¾ teaspoon ground turmeric
½ teaspoon ground ginger
¼ teaspoon vanilla bean paste
⅛ teaspoon cracked black pepper
⅛ teaspoon five-spice powder

Toasted Coconut Milk

2 cups (130 g/4 ½ oz) coconut flakes
3 cups (750 ml/1 ½ pints) filtered water
1 pinch of sea salt

Toppings

Toasted coconut flakes
Ground turmeric

To make the toasted coconut milk, place the coconut on a baking tray, pop into a 180°C (350°F) preheated oven and bake for about 4–5 minutes, or until golden and lightly toasted. Cool slightly before placing in a high-speed blender with the water and sea salt. Blitz until well combined, then strain through a nut milk bag into a clean glass container. Keeps refrigerated for 3–5 days and makes 3 cups (750 ml/1 ½ pints).

To make the golden latte, add all the ingredients into a small pot over medium-low heat. Bring to a simmer, whisking the ingredients together until warmed through to your liking.

Pour into a mug and top with some toasted coconut flakes and a little dusting of extra turmeric.

Hot

Mayan Hot Chocolate

Rich, smooth and spicy, this chilli-spiked hot chocolate has it all. Lush coconut milk is blended with dark chocolate and antioxidant-rich cacao powder for a double hit of chocolatey goodness.

1 ¼ cups (310 ml/10 ½ fl oz) coconut milk
50 g (1 ¾ oz) dark vegan chocolate, roughly chopped
1 small cinnamon stick
1 tablespoon agave syrup
2 teaspoons raw cacao powder
1 teaspoon maca powder
¼-½ teaspoon ancho chilli powder (as desired)
1 good pinch cayenne chilli powder

Whipped Coconut Cream

⅓ cup (80 ml/2 ½ fl oz) chilled coconut cream
3 teaspoons powdered sugar
¼ teaspoon vanilla bean paste or 1 good pinch ground cinnamon (optional)

Toppings

Whipped Coconut Cream
Vegan dark chocolate shavings
1 cinnamon stick
Cayenne chilli powder
Ground cinnamon

To make the whipped coconut cream, combine the ingredients in a small bowl and whisk for about 1-2 minutes until creamy and whipped.

To make the hot chocolate, place all the ingredients into a small pot over medium-low heat and bring to a simmer, whisking to combine. Simmer until the chocolate has melted and is warmed through to your liking.

Pour into a mug and top with whipped coconut cream, dark chocolate shavings, a cinnamon stick and a dusting of chilli powder and/or cinnamon.

Hot

It's Always Beets

Healthy, nutritious and oh-so-yummy, you can whip up this creamy pink latte in just a few minutes. Rose petals steeped in creamy homemade cashew milk get a hit of antioxidant-rich beetroot and cinnamon, which combine to make a delicately floral, caffeine-free alternative to your morning cup of coffee.

1 ¼ cups (310 ml/10 ½ fl oz) cashew milk
1 tablespoon organic edible rose petals
3 teaspoons beetroot powder
2 teaspoons maple syrup
½ teaspoon rosewater
¼ teaspoon vanilla bean paste
1-2 pinches ground cinnamon
1 tablespoon vegan collagen (optional)

Toppings
Organic edible rose petals
Freeze-dried raspberries, crushed
Beetroot powder

Place the cashew milk and rose petals in a small saucepan over medium heat and gently simmer for 2-3 minutes. Remove from the heat and let steep for 5-7 minutes.

Strain the milky rose tea into a high-speed blender and discard the petals. Add the beetroot powder, maple syrup, rosewater, vanilla bean paste and cinnamon into the blender, then blitz until well combined.

Return the rose latte to the saucepan and gently heat until warmed to your liking. Whisk in the collagen powder (if using).

Pour into a mug and serve with rose petals, freeze-dried raspberries and a pinch of beetroot powder.

The Holiday Special

The autumnal flavours of earthy pumpkin, nutty, buttery pecans and intoxicating spices cosy up together in this warming caffeine hit.

The pecan milk highlights the ginger, maple syrup and nutmeg, and the espresso packs a little punch for all you caffeine lovers who thrive on your morning jolt.

1 cup (250 ml/9 fl oz) pecan milk
2 tablespoons pumpkin, cooked and mashed
1 tablespoon maple syrup
1 teaspoon freshly grated ginger
¼ teaspoon ground cinnamon
¼ teaspoon vanilla bean paste
1 pinch freshly grated nutmeg
1 pinch ground cloves
1-2 shots (30-60 ml/1-2 fl oz) espresso (as desired)

Toppings
Coconut or vegan whipped cream
Dried orange slice
Cinnamon stick

Combine all the ingredients except the espresso in a small saucepan and place over low-medium heat. Whisk to combine, then simmer until warm, about 2-3 minutes.

Remove from the heat, add the espresso, and whisk to combine.

Pour into a large mug and serve with a dollop of whipped cream, a dried orange slice on top and a cinnamon stick on the side.

Hot

Hot

Blue Moon Milk

Sweet dreams are made of this ... This dream team of ingredients will have you dozing off peacefully before you even start counting sheep. Lavender flowers help treat insomnia and restlessness, blue pea flowers aid in reducing sleeplessness and stress, ashwagandha is an adaptogen that reduces anxiety, and almonds are a good source of magnesium and melatonin, both known to contribute to a restful slumber. Brew up a cup of this soothing moon milk and drift off into a good night's sleep.

1 ⅓ cups (330 ml/11 fl oz) almond milk

2 ½ teaspoons dried blue pea flowers

2 teaspoons maple or agave syrup

1 teaspoon culinary-grade organic lavender (or 1 lavender tea bag)

1 teaspoon ashwagandha powder

1 teaspoon cacao butter or coconut oil

¼ teaspoon vanilla bean paste

Toppings

Organic edible petals: violas, cornflower petals and/or lavender

Place the almond milk, blue pea flowers, maple (or agave) syrup and lavender into a small pot over medium-low heat. Bring to a simmer, then turn off and let steep for 5–7 minutes. Strain the milk into a high-speed blender, discarding the flowers. Place the remaining ingredients into the blender with the warm milk and blitz until combined and frothy.

Pour into your favourite cup, sprinkle with edible petals, and enjoy.

Hot

Gothic Detox

This concoction is dead sexy, intriguing and mysterious, just like Morticia herself. It combines earthy, nutty flavours with just a touch of exotic sweetness.

Activated charcoal is said to have detoxing capabilities, but don't overdo it—just a ½ teaspoon is enough. Adding extra collagen will keep your skin looking like it's never seen the sun.

You can also enjoy this latte over ice or with other milks, such as almond or sesame seed.

1 cup (250 ml/9 fl oz) hazelnut milk
3 tablespoons black tahini paste
2 teaspoons maple syrup
½ teaspoon organic activated coconut charcoal powder
¼ teaspoon vanilla bean paste
1 tablespoon vegan collagen powder (optional)
2 shots (60 ml/2 fl oz) espresso

Toppings
Black sesame seeds
1 vanilla bean, split

Place the milk, 1 ½ tablespoons black tahini paste, maple syrup, charcoal powder and vanilla into a small pot over medium-low heat and whisk to combine. Bring to a simmer and heat until warmed through, or to your liking. Pour into a high-speed blender, add the collagen (if using), and blitz until creamy and smooth.

Spoon the remaining 1 ½ tablespoons tahini into a glass or mug, pour in the blended hazelnut milk, and add the espresso shots. Finish with a sprinkle of black sesame seeds and a vanilla bean to garnish.

Hot

Hot

Magic Mocha Mushroom

This is a creamy, antioxidant-rich drink filled with health benefits and a delicious double hit of espresso. Creamy almond milk pairs well with the chocolatey, earthy flavours of coffee, cacao and mushroom powder.

The addition of medicinal mushrooms, such as chaga, reishi, cordyceps and lion's mane, bumps up the nutritional benefits of this morning heart-starter. These mushrooms have been used for centuries in traditional Chinese medicine. They are high in antioxidants and have a long list of health benefits, increasing energy and stamina, and supporting the immune system and brain health. You can find mushroom powders at your local health-food store or online.

½ cup (125 ml/4 fl oz) almond milk
1 tablespoon agave syrup
1 tablespoon raw cacao powder
½–1 teaspoon mixed or chaga mushroom powder (as desired)
2 shots (60 ml/2 fl oz) espresso
1 pinch ground cinnamon (optional)

Toppings

Coconut cream or vegan marshmallows
Cacao nibs
Raw cacao powder

Place the almond milk, agave syrup and cacao powder in a small pan over medium–low heat, and whisk to combine. Gently heat for about 2–3 minutes, then remove from the heat and whisk in the mushroom powder, espresso and cinnamon (if using).

Pour into a mug and top with coconut cream or marshmallows, cacao nibs and a little dusting of cacao powder.

Strawberry Fields

It doesn't need to be the height of strawberry season to enjoy this fruity, alcohol-infused milkshake. Frozen strawberries and strawberry liqueur blend with macadamia milk and ice cream into a delightfully boozy, dessert-y cocktail. Enjoy it simply as is, or fully loaded with a ribbon of whipped cream and fresh berries dusted with tart freeze-dried strawberries.

3 teaspoons strawberry
  jam
¼ cup (60 ml/2 fl oz)
  macadamia milk
1 ½ tablespoons vodka
1 ½ tablespoons
  strawberry liqueur
¼ cup (60 g/2 oz) frozen
  strawberries
1 scoop (55 g/2 oz) vegan
  vanilla ice cream
1 teaspoon Vanilla Syrup
  (see The Wake-Up Call
  recipe, page 70)

Toppings

Vegan whipped cream
Fresh strawberries
Crushed freeze-dried
  strawberries

Spoon the strawberry jam into the bottom of a chilled cocktail glass. Place the remaining ingredients into a high-speed blender and blitz until smooth and creamy. Pour the cocktail over the strawberry jam and garnish with whipped cream, fresh strawberries and a dusting of crushed freeze-dried strawberries.

Boozy

Luck Of The Irish

Chilled coffee with an Irish whiskey twist ... This boozy cold-brew cocktail is delicious, creamy and highly caffeinated. It's the perfect drink for a long, lazy brunch on a sunny day. You'll need to start this recipe a day before you want to serve it, because the coffee needs 12–24 hours to brew. For an extra caffeine hit, you can make your ice cubes with cold-brew coffee as well. The rich macadamia milk is offset by the whiskey and liqueurs.

Ice cubes or cold-brew ice cubes
⅓ cup (80 ml/2 ½ fl oz) chilled Cold-Brew Coffee
2 tablespoons chilled macadamia milk
1 ½ tablespoons Irish whiskey
1 ½ tablespoons vegan Irish cream liqueur
1 ½ tablespoons coffee liqueur
2 teaspoons agave syrup

Cold-Brew Coffee

1 cup (85 g/3 oz) coarsely ground coffee, use your favourite beans
4 cups (1 litre/2 pints) cold filtered water

Toppings

Vegan whipped cream
Crushed coffee beans

Make the cold-brew coffee the day before you wish to serve the iced Irish coffee. Place the ground coffee and water into a large glass container. Stir to combine, seal, and refrigerate for 12–24 hours. Strain the coffee through a paper coffee filter into a glass container, discarding the grounds. Keeps in the fridge for about 8 days and makes about 3 cups (750 ml/1 ½ pints).

To make cold-brew ice cubes, pour the cold-brew coffee into ice-cube trays and freeze for 4 hours or overnight, depending on the size of the cubes.

To make the Irish coffee, place the ice cubes into a glass and pour over the cold-brew coffee. Place the remaining ingredients into a cocktail shaker filled with ice and shake for 20–30 seconds until well chilled. Pour the mixture into the glass over the cold-brew coffee and garnish with whipped cream and a sprinkle of crushed coffee beans.

Choco-tini

Chocolate and hazelnuts are a match made in heaven. Warm, toasty, nutty hazelnut milk blends perfectly with bittersweet chocolate flavours in this martini. A little swirl of homemade chocolate syrup is a decadent addition, or you could replace it with a vegan chocolate hazelnut spread for a double dose of hazelnut goodness.

1 tablespoon Chocolate Syrup (see That's How the Cookie Crumbles recipe, page 58) or vegan chocolate hazelnut spread
Ice cubes
¼ cup (60 ml/2 fl oz) vegan dark chocolate liqueur
¼ cup (60 ml/2 fl oz) vodka
1 ½ tablespoons hazelnut milk

Topping
Vegan dark chocolate

Swirl the chocolate syrup into the bottom of a chilled martini glass.

Fill a cocktail shaker with ice, then add the chocolate liqueur, vodka and hazelnut milk. Seal and shake vigorously for about 20–30 seconds, or until chilled and frosty.

Strain into the prepared martini glass and garnish with a piece of dark chocolate.

Monkey Milk

This is a banana milkshake on steroids! Creamy macadamia milk teams up perfectly with vegan banana ice cream, crème de banana, vodka and coffee liqueur to make an adults-only, alcohol-spiked decadent drink that will have you swinging from the trees.

¼ cup (60 ml/2 fl oz) macadamia milk
2 tablespoons vodka
1 tablespoon crème de banana
1 tablespoon coffee liqueur
1 tablespoon crème de cacao
1 scoop (55 g/2 oz) vegan banana or vanilla ice cream
1 frozen banana, diced
2–3 ice cubes

Toppings

Banana slices
Vegan whipped cream
Freshly grated nutmeg

Place all the ingredients into a high-speed blender and blend for 20–40 seconds, or until well combined, smooth and frosty cold.

Pour the cocktail into a tall, chilled glass and garnish with banana slices, whipped cream and a pinch of freshly grated nutmeg to really bring out those sweet banana flavours.

Boozy

Love At Midnight

If you like piña coladas, you've got to try this one. Using homemade coconut milk, it seriously elevates the classic piña colada to a new level. Sweet, creamy and rich, this frosty, rum-laced, coconut-pineapple slushie will have you singing that 1970s number-one song while you catch the sunset.

¼ cup (60 ml/2 fl oz) coconut milk
⅔ cup (110 g/3 ¾ oz) diced frozen pineapple
¼ cup (60 ml/2 fl oz) chilled coconut cream
¼ cup (60 ml/2 fl oz) white rum
1 ½ tablespoons pineapple juice
2 tablespoons Vanilla Syrup (see The Wake-Up Call recipe, page 70)
1 cup ice cubes

Toppings
Pineapple wedge
Maraschino cherry
Paper umbrella

Place all the ingredients into a high-speed blender and blitz for about 30–40 seconds, or until slushy, frosty and smooth.

Pour into a chilled hurricane glass and top with a pineapple wedge and a maraschino cherry. Don't forget the paper umbrella!

Watermelon Coconut Kiss

Are you dreaming of swinging in a hammock as the trade winds breeze on by? This refreshing pink drink will have you feeling like you're on a tropical island, even if you're in your own backyard under the clothesline. Coconut milk, rum and watermelon taste like a sunny summer getaway in a glass, so pull out your Hawaiian shirt and ukulele, get blending and sip away into holiday mode.

⅓ cup (80 ml/2 ½ fl oz) coconut milk
2 cups (200 g/7 oz) frozen watermelon, diced
¼ cup (60 ml/2 fl oz) coconut rum
2 ½ teaspoons fresh lime juice
2 teaspoons agave syrup
2 large ice cubes

Toppings

Watermelon wedge
Coconut flakes
Lime disc
Orchid (optional)

Place all the ingredients into a high-speed blender and blitz for a few seconds, or until well combined, smooth and frosty.

Pour into a tall tiki glass and garnish with a watermelon wedge, coconut flakes, a lime disc and an orchid (if using). Serve with a straw and tall spoon, and dream away.

Left:
Watermelon
Coconut Kiss

Right: Love at
Midnight

Boozy

Eggless Eggnog

It's the holiday season. Are you dreaming of a white Christmas and a creamy vegan eggnog? Then this is the perfect recipe for you! Creamy cashew milk, thick vegan whipped cream and warming spices are all tied up into this pretty little package. Make it naughty with a good splash of bourbon, or keep it nice without the booze. Either way, it's lush and delicious.

⅔ cup (160 ml/5 ¼ fl oz) cashew milk

45 ml (1 ½ fl oz) bourbon whiskey

3 teaspoons maple syrup

⅛ teaspoon vanilla bean paste

1 good pinch each of ground allspice, ground cinnamon and freshly grated nutmeg

Toppings

Vegan whipped cream
Freshly grated nutmeg
Orange zest
Cinnamon stick

Fill a cocktail shaker with ice then add all the ingredients. Shake vigorously until chilled, frosty and well combined.

Pour the eggnog into an ice-filled double old-fashioned glass, then top with whipped cream, a fine grating of fresh nutmeg and orange zest. Add a cinnamon stick on the side.

Boozy

The Peanut Butter Cup

This is the perfect after-dinner cocktail when you want a little chocolatey sweet treat. Chocolate, roasted peanut butter and creamy macadamia milk blend into a chocolatey libation that tastes like your favourite confection. Out of macadamia milk? Use almond, Brazil nut or hazelnut milk as alternatives.

Take a minute to whip up this peanut butter lover's treat—you'll be happy you did!

Ice cubes
⅓ cup (80 ml/2 ½ fl oz) macadamia milk
45 ml (1 ½ fl oz) peanut butter whiskey
1 ½ tablespoons chocolate liqueur
2 teaspoons peanut butter
2 teaspoons Chocolate Syrup (see That's How the Cookie Crumbles recipe, page 58)

Glass Garnish
Chocolate Syrup
Salted roasted peanuts, finely crushed

To garnish your glass, place some chocolate syrup on a small saucer and some crushed peanuts on another saucer. Dip the rim of your cocktail glass into the chocolate, then into the crushed peanuts, making sure the glass rim is lightly covered in both chocolate and peanuts. Set aside.

Fill a cocktail shaker with ice cubes, then add the macadamia milk, peanut butter whiskey, chocolate liqueur, peanut butter and chocolate syrup. Shake vigorously for 20–30 seconds, or until well chilled and frosty.

Strain the cocktail into your garnished glass and enjoy.

Hazelnutty

The sweet, rich and nutty flavours of almond milk and hazelnut liqueur are naturally complementary. The almond milk enhances the hazelnut flavour, but you could double down and use hazelnut milk plus hazelnut liqueur for a full 'hazelnutty' experience. This is also delicious served as a soothing nightcap with warmed milk instead of ice.

Ice cubes
½ cup (125 ml/4 fl oz) almond or hazelnut milk
45 ml (1 ½ fl oz) hazelnut liqueur (Frangelico)
45 ml (1 ½ fl oz) vodka
1 teaspoon agave syrup

Topping
Toasted flaked almonds

Fill a cocktail shaker with ice cubes, then add the almond or hazelnut milk, hazelnut liqueur, vodka and agave syrup. Shake vigorously for about 20–30 seconds, or until chilled and frosty.

Place a single large ice cube in a double old-fashioned glass, pour the cocktail over the ice and serve sprinkled with a few toasted flaked almonds.

Boozy

After Dinner Mint

This is a minty, chocolatey dessert cocktail for the greenie in all of us. It's a perfect addition to your list of plant milk-based drinks.

The distinctive pistachio flavour shines through in this delightfully creamy, minty cocktail. It's rich and subtle, smooth and creamy all at the same time.

Ice cubes
¼ cup (60 ml/2 fl oz) pistachio milk
1 ½ tablespoons green crème de menthe
1 ½ tablespoons crème de cacao
1 ½ tablespoons vodka

Toppings

Vegan dark chocolate, shaved
Pistachio slivers
Fresh mint leaves

Fill a cocktail shaker with ice cubes, then add the pistachio milk, crème de menthe, crème de cacao and vodka. Shake vigorously for 20–30 seconds, or until chilled and frosty.

Pour into a chilled cocktail glass, then top with chocolate shavings, pistachio slivers and fresh mint leaves.

Boozy

Index

*Asterisk indicates booze content

T

U

V

W

Index

Acknowledgements

Thank you to Mark Campbell for bringing this project to me—it's always a great pleasure to work with you. Thanks also to Mietta Yans for your colourful, creative vision and Jess Cox for helping it all make sense. Thank you to photographer Armelle Habib for your talented eye and dedication to getting the perfect shot.

I'm so grateful for my family and friends, who are always incredibly helpful, encouraging and supportive towards my writing and cooking endeavours. Heartfelt thanks to Mom and Dad, Ann Marie, Jerry, Kathy and Tony, and also to Lorraine and Tommy, who all taste-tested the recipes and were especially interested in the boozy ones ... We had a lot of fun on the development road! And a huge special thank you to my brother Tony, who offered up his beautiful brand-new kitchen as my home base for recipe development and testing.

Harper *by* Design
An imprint of HarperCollins*Publishers*

HarperCollins*Publishers*
Australia • Brazil • Canada • France • Germany • Holland • India
Italy • Japan • Mexico • New Zealand • Poland • Spain • Sweden
Switzerland • United Kingdom • United States of America

HarperCollins acknowledges the Traditional Custodians of the land upon which we live and work,
and pays respect to Elders past and present.

First published in Australia in 2023
by HarperCollins*Publishers* Australia Pty Limited
Gadigal Country
Level 19, 201 Elizabeth Street, Sydney NSW 2000
ABN 36 009 913 517
harpercollins.com.au

A catalogue record for this book is available from the National Library of Australia.

ISBN 978 1 4607 6325 4

Publisher: Mark Campbell
Publishing Director: Brigitta Doyle
Editor: Jess Cox
Photographer: Armelle Habib
Stylist: Deborah Kaloper
Designer: Mietta Yans, HarperCollins Design Studio
Colour reproduction by Splitting Image Colour Studio, Clayton VIC
Printed and bound in China by RR Donnelley

8 7 6 5 4 3 2 1   23 24 25 26